Football Skills

T0364580

Contents

Written by Rachel Russ
Illustrated by Martin Bustamante

Collins

What are football skills?

In football, skills are the clever turns and tricks players do with the ball.

Skills help you to:

✓ control the ball

✓ speed past **opponents**

✓ have fun!

This book explains fast-footed skills to help you develop ball control and get past opponents.

Skills can help you play better football, but some people do skills just for fun.

Ball control

Controlling the ball is the most important skill in football.

This means gaining instant control of the ball and using both feet to travel with it.

How to do ... **toe taps**

1 Put one foot on top of the ball and the second foot flat on the ground.

2 Shift feet around.

3 Repeat, getting faster.

How to do ... **side sole rolls**

1 Roll the ball right with the sole of your right foot.

2 Roll the ball left with your left foot.

3 Repeat.

How to do ... **trapping**

1 Launch the ball up.

2 Use your foot to bring the ball to the ground and stop it.

Players can stop the ball with their chests.

Player profile: Sancho

- super speed with and without the ball

- lots of quick taps of the ball in a few seconds

- skills and speed help him to get past **defenders**

Out-skilling opponents

Skills can surprise opponents.

They help you to keep the ball and get past players as you travel, pass or **strike**.

Children are taught skills in training.

How to do ... **drag backs**

1 Put your stronger foot on top of the ball and your second foot at the side.

2 Roll back.

3 Go a different way.

How to do ... **stepovers**

1 Pretend you're going to kick the ball.

2 Swing your foot around the ball and step over it.

3 Kick it with your second foot.

How to do ... **a rabona**

To do a rabona (ra-boa-na) you kick the ball under your own standing leg.

A rabona is a bit like kicking the ball cross-legged!

Player profile: Marta

- **flair**, quick feet and super skill with the ball
- non-stop tricks, turns and skills to **perplex** defenders
- fast runner
- gets lots of goals!
- raw talent

Focus on: Panna

Panna is a sort of football game. It is played one against one. To win, you nutmeg your opponent.

Nutmeg: kick the ball out under your opponent's legs.

Glossary

defenders players that protect their team's goal

flair skill and talent

opponents players on the team you are playing against

perplex confuse

strike attempt to kick the ball into the goal

Index

Top skills!

Ball control

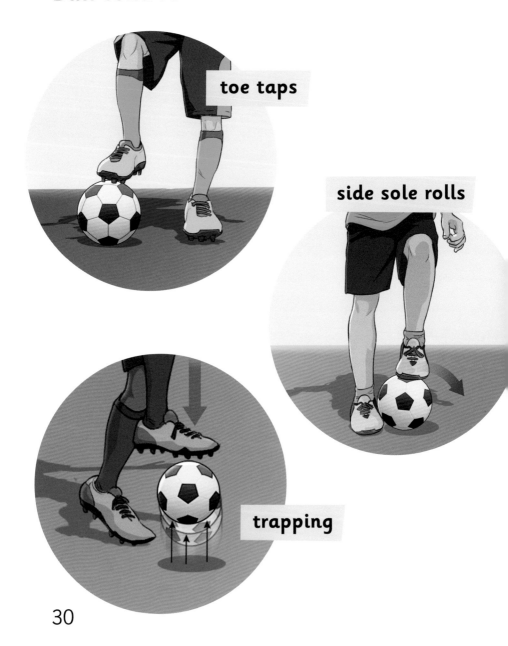

toe taps

side sole rolls

trapping

Out-skilling opponents

drag backs

stepovers

rabona

After reading

Letters and Sounds: Phase 5

Word count: 396

Focus phonemes: /ai/ ay, ey /ee/ ea /igh/ i-e, i /oa/ o, oe, ow, o-e /oo/ ew, ou, u, u-e /ar/ a /ow/ ou /or/ al, our, augh, aw, au

Common exception words: of, to, the, put, are, have, do, what, their, people, some, into, one, be

Curriculum links: Physical Education

National Curriculum learning objectives: Reading/word reading: apply phonic knowledge and skills as the route to decode words; read accurately by blending sounds in unfamiliar words containing GPCs that have been taught; Reading/comprehension (KS2): understand what they read, in books they can read independently, by checking that the text makes sense to them, discussing their understanding and explaining the meaning of words in context; identifying main ideas drawn from more than one paragraph and summarising these, identifying how language, structure, and presentation contribute to meaning

Developing fluency

- Take turns reading a page. Check that your child pauses at commas, ellipses and bullet points in lists.

Phonic practice

- Focus on spellings of /or/ and /ow/ sounds. Ask your child to sound out and blend the following words:

  around   raw   ground   football   without

- Can your child identify whether the following words contain the /ow/ sound or the /or/ sound?

  tour (*or*)   shout (*ow*)   four (*or*)   proud (*ow*)

Extending vocabulary

- Look at page 14 and point to the words **super speed**. Ask your child to think of a phrase or word with a similar meaning. (e.g. *fast moving, lightning motion*)

- Repeat for the following:

  page 2: clever (e.g. *brilliant, smart*)
  page 6: controlling (e.g. *being in charge of, directing*)
  page 24: flair (e.g. *gift, instinct*)